Robert
Boyle

Robert Boyle

Father of Chemistry

John Allen

BLACKBIRCH PRESS
An imprint of Thomson Gale, a part of The Thomson Corporation

THOMSON
GALE

Detroit • New York • San Francisco • San Diego • New Haven, Conn.
Waterville, Maine • London • Munich

Photo Credits:
Cover: © Stefano Bianchetti/CORBIS
© HIP/Art Resource, N.Y., 43
© Erich Lessing/Art Resource, N.Y., 16, 37, 51
© Reunion des Musees Nationaux/Art Resource, N.Y., 49
© SCALA/Art Resource, N.Y., 30
© Tate Gallery/Art Resource, N.Y., 33
© Archivo Iconografico,S.A./CORBIS, 15
© Bettmann/CORBIS, 25, 28, 33, 38, 39
© Stefano Bianchetti/CORBIS, 19, 45
© Historical Picture Archive/CORBIS, 13
© David Lees/CORBIS, 29, 40
© Michael Nicholson/CORBIS, 35
© Hulton Archive by Getty Images, 42, 47, 52
© Richard Cummins/Lonely Planet Images, 9
© Lee Foster/Lonely Planet Images, 10
Photos.com, 46, 57
Photo Researchers, Inc., 54
Stock Montage, Inc, 7, 12, 27

LIBRARY OF CONGRESS CATALOGING-IN-PUBLICATION DATA

Allen, John.
  Robert Boyle / by John Allen.
    p. cm. — (Giants of science)
  Includes bibliographical references and index.
  ISBN 1-56711-887-9 (hardcover : alk. paper)
  1. Boyle, Robert, 1627-1691—Juvenile literature. 2. Scientists—Great Britain—Biography—Juvenile literature. I. Title. II. Series.

  Q143.B77A79 2005
  509.2—dc22   2004020017

CONTENTS

An Exhibition Among

    Scientists 6

Robert Boyle's Legacy 8

Birth and Early Childhood 8

Education at Eton 11

Uncertain Health 12

The Grand Tour 13

A Life-Changing Event 14

Italy and Galileo 15

The Irish Rebellion 17

England and Civil War 18

Secluded Life at Stalbridge . . .20

Scientific Beginnings 21

A Fortune in Ireland 22

The Invisible College 23

The Great Assistant 24

An Improved Air Pump 25

A Simple Test 27

A Candle in a Vacuum 27

Magnetism, Light, and Sound .28

Three Years of Experiments . .29

The Pressure of the

    Atmosphere 30

Weighing Air 32

A Great Book of Science 34

Boyle's Law 35

A Bout with Controversy 36

The Skeptical Chemist 37

The Royal Society 38

Back to the Laboratory 40

The Plague and

    the Great Fire 42

Back to London 44

The Litmus Test 46

Gunpowder Under Water 47

Definition of an Element 48

Study of Alchemy 50

A Terrible Setback 50

Europe's Great Scientist 53

An Honor Declined 55

Final Years 55

The Great Experimenter 56

Influence on His Age 57

Important Dates 58

Notes 60

Glossary 61

For More Information 62

Index 63

An Exhibition Among Scientists

Robert Boyle prided himself on controlling his emotions, but he could not avoid a feeling of excitement. His work with a new device—an air pump that could create a vacuum—was the sort of scientific breakthrough he had dreamed of as a boy. Now he would share his experiments with the members of a group of scientists called the Invisible College—the forerunner of the Royal Society of London.

Boyle invited the group to assemble at his laboratory. With the help of his assistant, Robert Hooke, he re-created some tests they had performed with the air pump. A lamb's bladder placed in the pump's sealed glass bowl expanded then popped as air was pumped out. The ticking of a watch inside the bowl grew faint and finally silent as air was removed. A burning candle was extinguished. Every experiment was done flawlessly.

The members were impressed not only with the experiments but also with the ingenious apparatus itself. Boyle readily admitted that most of the credit for the air pump belonged to Hooke. The assembled scientists also approved of Boyle's meticulous procedures. Such careful work fit in well with the group's new ideas about the importance of tests and observation in science, in place of pure theory and guesswork.

As the grand finale for the evening, Boyle performed a test that was first suggested in the writings of the great Italian scientist Galileo Galilei. Inside a long glass tube he placed a feather and a piece of lead. With the air pump, Hooke created a vacuum in the tube. Then Boyle quickly turned the tube upside down. The lead and the feather fell side by side, striking the bottom of the tube at the same instant. As Galileo had suggested, objects in a vacuum fall at the same rate.

The members of the Invisible College applauded Boyle and his fascinating work. He had proved that he was not merely a talented amateur but also a genuine scientist in his own right.

Robert Boyle's experiments with an air pump that created a vacuum impressed fellow scientists.

Robert Boyle's Legacy

Boyle lived at a time when rational thought was rapidly replacing ingrained ideas and superstition in everyday life. Before him, scientists relied heavily on the authority of ancient thinkers and only rarely challenged the old conclusions with their own experiments. Boyle changed all that by insisting on the importance of controlled experiments as the basis for modern science.

Many of Boyle's discoveries in chemistry and physics were groundbreaking. For example, his use of the air pump to study the qualities of air and a vacuum virtually opened a new field. In addition, he invented many new tools for the laboratory, including a pocket thermometer, an improved barometer, a hydrometer for measuring the density of liquids, a pressure cooker, and even a sulfur-tipped match.

Perhaps Boyle's greatest influence on scientists of today is his methodical approach to experiments. He assembled the first "research team," performed each of his experiments with meticulous care, and always noted the result, whether it was a success or a failure. Boyle's procedures led to a culture of science in which each generation could build on the work of its predecessors.

The story of Boyle's life begins far from his later homes in Oxford and London. It starts with his birth in Ireland to a family of wealth and privilege—a background that would eventually help him to concentrate on a scientific career.

> "He [Richard Boyle, the Earl of Cork], by God's blessing on his prosperous industry, from very inconsiderable beginnings, built so plentiful and so eminent a fortune, that his prosperity has found many admirers, but few parallels."
>
> ROBERT BOYLE, "AN ACCOUNT OF PHILARETUS"

Birth and Early Childhood

On January 25, 1627, Robert Boyle was born at Lismore Castle in Ireland. He was the fourteenth child of the Boyle family and the youngest son. His father, Richard, was at the height of an extraordinary career. Having journeyed to Ireland at age 22

Robert Boyle was born at Lismore Castle (above) in Ireland in January 1627.

with only a few pounds in his pocket, Richard Boyle had married the daughter of a wealthy Irish family, made shrewd land purchases, and set up iron-smelting and linen-weaving industries. Eventually, he became the wealthiest Englishman in the country. His landholdings in Ireland were second to none, and the English Crown had made him the first Earl of Cork.

The earl believed that his sons should live away from ease and luxury until it was time to begin their formal education. When Robert was six months old, he was sent to live in the simple cottage of a peasant woman. During this time, Robert's mother passed away in Dublin, Ireland, following complications from childbirth. Robert never knew her.

When he was four, Robert returned to Lismore. The next years were crowded with happiness. From a host of tutors he learned English, French, and Latin, along with skills such as horseback riding. Robert's older sister Katherine looked after him with motherly affection. When the earl noticed that his youngest son was passionate about books, he brought the boy

Boyle began studying at Eton College, an English boarding school near London, at the age of eight.

volumes from his travels. Once Robert got to join his father on a tour of his lands in Ireland. The earl saw something special in the boy and determined to give him every opportunity to improve himself.

Education at Eton

Robert was eight when he and his brother Francis entered Eton, a renowned English boarding school near London. Robert had good fortune in the scholars who instructed him at Eton. The provost of the school was Sir Henry Wotton, a cultured man and former ambassador to Italy. The headmaster, John Harrison, oversaw a curriculum that kept students busy from dawn to dark. Studies included Bible reading, Latin, arithmetic, history, and logic. Young scholars were also expected to participate in sports such as rowing, rugby, and cricket. However, Robert disliked sports and preferred to read whenever he had a spare moment.

"My Brother,
It has pleased God to bring us safe to Oxford, and I am lodged at Mr. Crosse's, with design to be able to give you from experience an account which is the warmest room; and indeed I am satisfied with neither of them as to that point, because the doors are placed so just by the chimnies, that if you have the benefit of the fire, you must venture having the inconvenience of the wind.

FROM A LETTER TO BOYLE FROM HIS SISTER KATHERINE

Wotton took a personal interest in Eton's most promising students. He would invite a group of boys to dinner in order to test them in debate. Wotton himself was interested in science, or "natural philosophy" as it was then called. One evening he introduced Robert and some other students to an important new idea—the experimental method. Instead of trusting blindly in old books, some scientists were beginning to test theories with careful experiments. Robert grew excited at Wotton's words. Helped by his reading and his quick mind, the boy had developed a rabid curiosity about the world. He

Galen (above) was considered an authority on human anatomy even though he based his observations on the study of animals.

dreamed of someday unlocking its secrets with his own scientific work.

In Robert Boyle's time, works by classical Greek authors such as Aristotle and Hippocrates were considered the last word on most topics. Their observations and conclusions were rarely challenged. For example, Galen, a Greek who lived around A.D. 150, wrote many books on anatomy. He had dissected animals such as dogs and goats to study the structure of their bodies. Even though many of his observations did not hold true for human anatomy, Galen still was considered the ultimate authority on the subject. Physicians saw no need to duplicate his time-consuming dissections. This attitude prevailed in almost every branch of knowledge: Why revisit questions that the ancients had already settled?

At Eton, Robert read the same classical authors as the other students did. However, Wotton supplemented the boy's reading with more modern works from his own library. Books by Galileo and Johannes Kepler, a German astronomer, kindled Robert's imagination with new ideas about the universe and man's place within it. Robert learned that human knowledge was a never-ending quest.

Uncertain Health

Robert's time at Eton was also marked by several bouts of ill health. His frail constitution could barely cope with the school's difficult schedule of classes, devotions, and athletics. He often suffered from fevers and stomach problems. The crude medical practices of the day only made things worse. Once, while living in the headmaster's house, Robert was having trouble recovering from a bout with fever. The doctor sent for a potion from the local apothecary. When Robert drank it, he felt as if his stomach were going to burst. He became violently ill but recovered at last. He had been given the wrong medicine.

Robert's health was not the only challenge he faced at school. He had a persistent stammer that grew worse whenever he became excited. This stammer only increased his tendency to shyness. Despite these problems and his lack of enthusiasm for games, Robert was popular among the other students. His honest, straightforward manner and genuine love of knowledge earned their respect.

The Grand Tour

After three years at Eton, Robert and Francis embarked on the next stage of their education. In October 1639 they began a long tour of Europe. The earl hired a fiery Frenchman named Isaac Marcombes to accompany them as their tutor. Twelve-year-old Robert was thrilled at this chance to see the world.

Robert Boyle, his brother, and their tutor stayed for several months in Geneva, Switzerland, while on their European tour.

First the party crossed the rough seas of the English Channel. In France, they made their way on horseback along the Seine River to Paris. From there they traveled to Lyons and then crossed the Alps to reach Geneva, Switzerland.

The Boyles and their tutor remained in Geneva for several months. The main reason was that, unbeknownst to the earl, Marcombes had a wife and children in the city. Throughout a severe winter, Robert and Francis lived and worked in the Marcombes's home. Among other subjects, they studied Latin grammar, logic, geography, history, and geometry. For exercise, the boys fenced and played paddle tennis. Robert enjoyed the warm fires and cozy atmosphere of his tutor's house, but he and his brother were already longing for new sights and experiences.

> "I am not ambitious to appear a man of letters: I could be content the world should think I had scarce looked upon any other book than that of nature."
>
> ROBERT BOYLE, FROM *THE PHILOSOPHICAL WORKS OF ROBERT BOYLE* (1738)

A Life-Changing Event

In the spring Marcombes led his charges on a horseback journey high in the Alps. One night, while staying at a château, or plush hotel, Robert was awakened by a deafening thunderclap. From his window he observed a storm like none he had ever seen before. Gigantic streaks of lightning split the sky and illuminated the château's courtyard like daylight. Trees bent almost double from the fierce winds. Thunder rumbled again and again, shaking the timbers of the château and rattling the windowpanes.

Young Robert grew terrified. Was this the Day of Judgment, he asked himself? Robert had always been religious, but now, in his frightened state during the storm, he vowed to make his Protestant faith the focal point of his life. As he put it in his autobiography (written in the third person), "All further additions to his life should be more Religiously & carefully employ'd."[1]

Robert realized that a promise made under duress might lack the strength of true conviction. The next day, with the dangers of the thunderstorm safely past, he repeated his promise to God. A new sense of purpose filled Robert. He felt he must do something important with his life—but exactly what he had yet to decide.

Italy and Galileo

One possible career path was linked to Robert's new desire. He and his brother begged their tutor to let them travel to Italy. With his interest in science, Robert had a special motive to visit Italy. The elderly Galileo Galilei, the world's most celebrated

Galileo Galilei dictates to his secretary. The famous scientist died before Boyle had a chance to meet him.

Galileo defends himself at his trial for going against the teachings of the Catholic Church.

scientist, lived in a village near Florence. With luck, Robert would be able to meet his hero.

Initially, however, his hopes were dashed. In a letter to Marcombes, the boys' father rejected the idea, insisting that Italy at present was too dangerous for English travelers. Anti-English passions were running high among Italians since a London mob had killed an Italian priest in the streets. For the second year in a row, the Boyles spent the winter in Geneva.

Finally, Marcombes and the young Boyles received permission to go. For safety reasons, they would pose as French travelers and speak only French and Italian. As an additional aid, Marcombes obtained from the earl a letter signed by the English monarch, Charles I. The letter requested all kings, high officials, and other authorities to protect the visitors and treat them well.

In September 1641, the trio crossed the Alps into Italy. They visited cities whose names, familiar from Robert's vast reading, held a poetic ring for him, including Verona, Padua, and Venice. At night Robert read from Galileo's works. He admired the way that Galileo built his theories from observations he had made himself with his telescope. The Italian was quite ready to contradict the ancient writers if his own results demanded it. For example, Aristotle had declared that all the heavenly bodies were flawless. Galileo discovered that the moon's surface was pocked with craters and the sun contained dark spots. Most dangerously of all, Galileo maintained that Nicolaus Copernicus, a Polish astronomer, was correct: The Sun, and not the Earth, was the center around which the bodies of the solar system revolved. For this conclusion, which contradicted the teachings of the Catholic Church, Galileo had been placed under house arrest by church authorities. Now old and almost blind, he had been confined to his village for eight years.

Robert's party spent the winter in Florence, admiring the city's art and architecture. As much as Robert enjoyed the sights, his mind kept circling back to Galileo. Robert hoped that the letter from Charles I would gain them an interview with the great man. His hopes were dashed when Galileo died in January before the meeting could be arranged. Robert's disappointment, however, quickly changed to determination. In his journals, he had begun to call himself *Philaretus*, which meant "lover of truth." Like his hero Galileo, he would devote his life to science and seek the truth about the world.

The Irish Rebellion

After a visit to Rome, Robert's group was ready to start homeward. By sailboat and then on foot, they traveled back to the port of Marseilles, arriving in May 1642. Waiting for them there was an urgent letter from the boys' father. The earl's estates had been attacked by Irish rebels as part of a larger rebellion against the English in Ireland. Richard Boyle had depleted his fortune in a desperate attempt to arm other English landowners against the rebels. He had sold the household silver to provide his sons with 250 pounds for the journey home. However, the letter included no bill of exchange for that sum. Evidently, the earl's agent in London had taken the money for himself. Robert and his brother lacked the means to get home.

With the help of a small loan from Marcombes, Francis was able to return to Ireland. He arrived in time to fight in the Battle of Liscarrol alongside his brothers, one of whom died in the fighting. As for Robert, his ill health ruled out the notion of following Francis. Instead he accompanied Marcombes back to Geneva.

While in Geneva, Robert learned the fate of his father. In September 1643, Charles I signed a treaty with the rebels. One of its stipulations was that the Earl of Cork had to surrender Lismore Castle to the Irish. The earl died, broken and almost penniless, at the same time the treaty was being signed. It was almost a year before Robert was able to leave Geneva. When he finally had enough money for the journey, he decided to go to England. For the moment, Ireland held too many painful memories. Perhaps in London he could make a fresh start.

England and Civil War

As seventeen-year-old Robert walked the streets of London, he had no friends, almost no money, and few prospects. Shortly after arriving, he was reunited with his sister Katherine. In the

This banner supports the Parlimentarian cause in the English civil war.

intervening years she had married a viscount and was now Lady Ranelagh. At once she resumed the maternal role she had played in Robert's life after the death of their mother. Katherine insisted that Robert come live with her and her four children.

At the time of Boyle's return, England was plunged in the chaos of civil war. The conflict was between the Royalists, who backed King Charles I, and the Parliamentarians, including members of the elected Parliament and their

Boyle was troubled by the English civil war but tried not to take sides.

supporters. Years before, the king had dissolved Parliament in an attempt to rule by royal decree. Resentment grew as Charles introduced unpopular church reforms and levied unfair taxes. The king's disputes with the legislature quickly escalated into armed conflict. By 1644, Charles's court had moved to Oxford, while Parliament, with the support of many who sought stability, continued to collect taxes and make laws for the country. Neither side could yet gain a decisive military victory.

The war troubled Boyle, though he tried not to take sides. His father had been an outspoken Royalist. Now he found that his sister Katherine was solidly behind the Parliamentary cause. As for Boyle, he only wanted to settle at Stalbridge, the English estate he had inherited from his father. The civil war made even that goal difficult to reach. In a letter to a friend, he wrote: "[I] got safe into England towards the middle of the year 1644, where we found things in such a confusion, that although the manor of Stalbridge were by my father's decease descended unto me, yet it was near four months before I could get thither."[2]

As it turned out, it was Katherine who helped Boyle obtain his estate at Stalbridge. She introduced him to a powerful member of Parliament. This person was able to help Boyle secure the title to his properties in England and Ireland. He also arranged for Boyle's safe passage to the south of England, where Stalbridge was located. Robert was appalled at the state of the property, with its weed-choked fields, untended orchards, and ruined manor house. He wasted no time making repairs and improvements. He found a reliable manager and rented cottages to experienced tenant farmers. By autumn of 1646 the estate was running smoothly and its crops were profitable.

Secluded Life at Stalbridge

Boyle's years at Stalbridge marked the beginning of his career as a writer and scientist. However, his first writings were about religion and ethics, not science. He tried many different genres, including autobiography, poetry, fictional biography, and speeches.

The most famous of these productions is *Seraphic Love*, a book-length letter to an imaginary friend who has been disappointed in love. Boyle instructs the friend about the pains and uncertainties of human love, and advises him to concentrate on a higher form of love—a devotion to God. Although Boyle wrote the book for private distribution, he eventually published it in 1659. With its stilted style, *Seraphic Love* is no longer read today, but in Boyle's time it went through nine editions and was translated into three languages.

Secluded on his estate, Boyle had little to think about except his writing and his many health problems. His eyesight was bad, his digestion worse,

1. To frame a good Hypothesis, one must see First, that it clearly intelligible be.

2. Next that it nought assume, nor do suppose That flatly does any known Truth oppose.

3. Thirdly, that with itself it do consist So that no One part, the other do resist.

ROBERT BOYLE,
FROM HIS NOTEBOOKS

and he caught cold easily. He suffered from frequent fevers and was wracked by the pain of kidney stones. An interest in chemistry books led him to prepare drugs for himself. Some of his recipes came from books on alchemy, a mystical forerunner to chemistry, or from his own trial and error. He had no qualms about trying these new medicines, rating them in his journals according to their effectiveness. Some of Boyle's attempted cures were primitive indeed. He placed a ring carved from the hoof of an elk on his bedside table to protect him from stomach cramps. He also hung a sheep's gallbladder over the bed to cure jaundice.

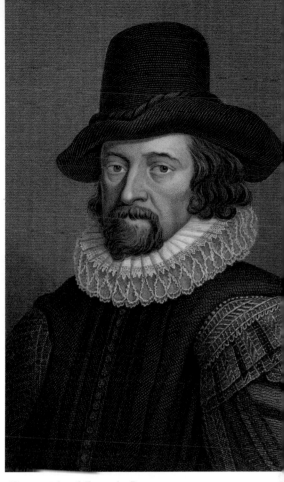

The work of Francis Bacon (above) and other scientists inspired Boyle to develop his own theories.

Scientific Beginnings

Influenced by his reading, Boyle took an interest in scientific experiments. The ideas of physical scientists such as Francis Bacon, Pierre Gassendi, René Descartes, and Galileo gave him a passionate interest in exploring the makeup of the physical world. From their works on physics, he read theories about the movement of the planets, the circulation of blood, and the relationship of air and vacuum, or absence of air. He hoped that someday he would offer the world of science great theories of his own.

Soon he set about building his own laboratory at Stalbridge. He ordered various crucibles, retorts, and other glass vessels for condensing and distilling substances by heat. He sent for chemicals, metals, and acids. Isolated as he was, he had difficulty obtaining some equipment, such as a furnace for heating compounds. One furnace arrived broken in pieces. Finally, Boyle journeyed to the Netherlands and brought back a furnace himself.

Boyle amused himself by making all sorts of chemical tests—whatever his agile mind could conceive. His letters and papers refer to his use of a microscope to study the structure of living things. He repeated many experiments from books, carefully noting the results. He mixed, charred, pulverized, liquefied, boiled, and strained different kinds of matter. Some of his work had the sophistication of true chemistry, and some had the superstitious taint of folk remedies and magical potions. Boyle also performed simple dissections and studied the circulation of blood.

From the start Boyle was fascinated with his new work. By August 31, 1649, he described himself in a letter to Katherine as "so transported and bewitched [as to] fancy my laboratory a kind of Elysium"[3]—or paradise. Boyle saw his experiments as a means of discovering the truth about God's creation. The promise he had made during that long-ago thunderstorm carried through to his scientific work as well.

A Fortune in Ireland

Soon, the affairs of state again played an important part in Boyle's life. Charles I was beheaded by Parliament in 1649, and a year later his son Charles II tried to renew the fight in Scotland. Parliamentary forces, led by Oliver Cromwell, twice defeated armies of Royalist Scots. In 1652, Boyle, concerned by the general unrest, traveled to Ireland to see about the few properties still held in the family name. That year, Cromwell defeated the Irish army as well and proceeded to divide Irish lands among the English landowners. As a reward for staunch support, Cromwell restored to the Boyle family the earl's old estates. As a result, Robert Boyle received properties whose rents reached 3,000 pounds a year.

Boyle was now extremely wealthy, just as his father had been. This turned out to be a boon for science. As a gentleman of leisure, Boyle could devote himself to his scientific work.

Oliver Cromwell and his Parliamentary forces (pictured) defeated the Royalist Scot armies twice.

The Invisible College

On a visit to London in 1653, Boyle met John Wilkins, a doctor who had just been named warden of Wadham College at Oxford University. Wilkins was the leader of a group of scientists referred to as the Invisible College. These men shared an interest in what they called "experimental philosophy," or scientific experiments. Since 1645 they had met weekly to discuss their work and share ideas. The meetings began in London, but with the onset of the civil war, many members had moved to Oxford. Cromwell had appointed many of them to posts at the university.

Boyle had first met the scientists of the Invisible College when he was living with his sister Katherine. Now Wilkins strongly urged Boyle to join the group in Oxford and live in college rooms. Certainly the thought of living and working among fellow scientists was appealing to Boyle. Yet he preferred to remain separate from the university.

23

John Wilkins of Oxford's Wadham College (pictured) convinced Boyle in a 1653 meeting to join other scientists in work at Oxford.

He enlisted Katherine to locate rooms in Oxford. She soon found him lodgings with an apothecary named John Crosse. With a motherly eye for Boyle's always-delicate health, Katherine made sure that the rooms were not chilly or drafty.

Boyle was eager to renew his acquaintanceships with the members of the Invisible College. He was alive with plans and ideas that could flourish in the intellectual atmosphere of Oxford. Now his real work would begin.

The Great Assistant

In the summer of 1654, Robert Boyle established himself as a full-time "natural philosopher," or scientist. A crew of workers hauled crates of his equipment into Crosse's apothecary. Once his laboratory was set up, Boyle began gathering assistants for his work.

One of his first needs was a "chemical tutor" to instruct him and his assistants in the rules of practical chemistry. Boyle wanted to be sure that his men knew the proper ways to handle chemicals and laboratory apparatus. For this job, he hired an Oxford expert, Peter Stahl.

Most important, Boyle needed a clever head assistant, a young man willing to tackle a variety of problems. Wilkins suggested a student named Robert Hooke. Unlike most other Oxford students, who came from rich families, Hooke was an orphan who had to wait tables for other students in order to pay his tuition. A childhood bout with smallpox had left him scarred and stunted. He had a twisted body and shrunken limbs. Headaches and other pains made it difficult for him to sleep. As a result, he would stay up late into the night reading and working.

Work was the obsession of Robert Hooke's life. He had a genius for mechanical objects and could design and build almost anything. His curiosity in all fields of science matched Boyle's own. Boyle recognized Hooke's promise immediately and hired him as his paid assistant.

Robert Hooke used this microscope while working as Boyle's assistant.

An Improved Air Pump

One of the first assignments that Boyle gave his new assistant was to build an improved air pump. The idea sprang from a celebrated experiment that Boyle had read about. A German named Otto von Guericke had designed a device that could pump air out of a container.

First, von Guericke had fitted two large copper bowls together to make a complete sphere and then sealed the seam with wax. Next, his pump was employed to remove the air from the copper sphere through a pipe attached to one of the bowls. Two teams of eight horses were lashed to the bowls, one team to each half of the sphere. The horses could not pull the bowls apart. However, when von Guericke pumped air back into the sphere, the two halves fell apart at once.

Boyle understood that von Guericke's experiment was an example of air pressure. When the air was removed from inside the sphere, the pressure of the air outside held the two halves together with a powerful suction. Pumping air back in equalized the air pressure inside and out, and the bowls fell apart.

While he admired the ingenuity of von Guericke's test, Boyle thought that his air pump was inadequate. It had to be used in water to prevent air from escaping. Also, Boyle wanted a clear glass bowl for his experiments, instead of the copper sphere that von Guericke had used. Boyle described to Hooke the precise features he would like to have in a new air pump fit for the laboratory.

Hooke threw himself into the task with single-minded fervor. In a short time, he presented his air pump to Boyle. It had an eight-gallon glass bowl so that Boyle could easily see objects inside. Pistons and pumps were connected to the bowl with brass pipes. Crude leather valves allowed air to pass one way but not the other. While von Guericke's pump had required the strenuous efforts of two individuals, Hooke's pump could easily be operated by one person. Hooke's first pump was makeshift, but it could be used to create a vacuum more effectively than any other device then in existence.

"Using a J-shaped tube Boyle showed that if he compressed air twice as strongly as usual he could produce twice as strong a spring. He concluded that the process could go on indefinitely, so that there were no limits to the power of the air's spring.

STEVEN SHAPIN AND SIMON SCHAFFER, *LEVIATHAN AND THE AIR-PUMP: HOBBES, BOYLE AND THE EXPERIMENTAL LIFE* (1985)

A Simple Test

Now that Boyle had his air pump, his brain teemed with experiments to try. First, however, he devised a simple test of the apparatus. He took an elastic lamb's bladder, much like a balloon, and filled it with air. He tied off the bladder and placed it inside the glass bowl of the air pump, then plugged the bowl shut. An assistant raised and lowered the piston arm to remove the air from the bowl. With each downstroke of the piston, the bladder

Robert Boyle and his assistant discuss air pressure in Boyle's laboratory.

swelled until it almost doubled in size. Finally, it burst.

Boyle was pleased with the operation of the pump. By creating a vacuum, Boyle had refuted an ancient belief that "nature abhors a vacuum"—that a vacuum could not, in fact, exist. He was also satisfied at his demonstration of the result of air pressure. When the bladder was sitting in the sealed bowl, the air pressure inside the bladder was equal to the air pressure in the bowl. As the air in the bowl was removed, the air in the bladder could expand. Finally it expanded to the point where the rubbery bladder burst.

A Candle in a Vacuum

One of Boyle's next experiments was to see if a candle would burn in a vacuum. First he lowered a lit candle into the air-filled glass bowl by means of a thin wire. Then he replaced the stopper and observed, with an eye on his watch. The bowl slowly filled with smoke and eventually, in about five minutes, the flame burned out.

Boyle relit the candle and repeated the procedure, this time ordering an assistant to pump out the air in the bowl. How would the candle flame react in a vacuum? The flame went out in less than a minute.

From this experiment, Boyle deduced that air, or something in air, was necessary for burning. In his meticulous notes, he also recorded that the candle's smoke did not rise in the vacuum, but fell.

Boyle also tried placing a piece of glowing coal in the glass bowl. The glow disappeared when air was let out, but returned, if the coal was still hot, when air was pumped back in. Again Boyle was struck by the necessity of air for combustion to occur.

Magnetism, Light, and Sound

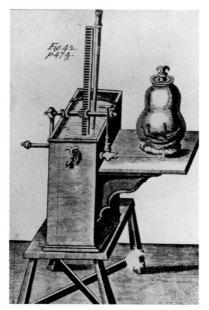

Boyle used this vacuum pump he invented to do breathing experiments with animals and insects.

Among Boyle's carefully numbered experiments were tests of different forces in an absence of air. He placed a compass inside the bowl and touched a magnet to the outside of the glass. The magnet attracted the compass needle as he knew it would. But would the magnetic force operate across a vacuum? He repeated the experiment with the air removed from the bowl. Again the compass needle swayed to the magnet. A vacuum obviously had no effect on magnetism. He also found that light could travel in a vacuum. Objects in the bowl appeared no different whether there was air inside or not.

Experiments with sound brought interesting results. Using a string, Hooke lowered his large pocket watch into the bowl with its cover open, so that its working parts were in view. The watch was ideal for the experiment because of the loud ticking sound it made.

With the stopper closed, Hooke operated the pump. As air left the bowl, the audible ticking of the watch gradually grew fainter. Finally, the sound could not be heard. Yet the watch's mechanism was still working.

To complete the experiment, Boyle had Hooke gradually replace the air in the glass bowl. The ticking sound returned, faintly at first and then at its regular level. Boyle was intrigued. He noted that sound was impossible in a vacuum.

Boyle also tested for breathing in a vacuum. A mouse placed in the glass bowl expired when the air was removed, suggesting that air was indispensable to life. Insects, however, continued to move about. Apparently they did not require air the same way animals did.

Three Years of Experiments

Boyle's new air pump led him to perform a series of experiments that lasted three years. In his day, little was known about the composition and nature of air and other gases. Few were doing work in this area, and most scientists simply accepted the age-old theories of Aristotle and other classical thinkers. With his effective air pump or vacuum chamber, Boyle was able to explore a whole new field of science. He was especially intrigued by air's elasticity, or, as he phrased it in a later book title, "the spring of the air."

One predecessor who had done work with air pressure was Galileo's assistant, Evangelista Torricelli. In his most

Above is a twentieth-century model of Evangelista Torricelli's mercury barometer.

Torricelli demonstrates his mercury barometer. The result of his experiment caused disagreement among other scientists.

famous experiment, Torricelli had made a kind of mercury barometer. To begin, he had partially filled a long glass tube with mercury. The tube was open only at one end. Closing the open end with his finger, Torricelli had tipped the tube upside down and lowered it into a dish also filled with mercury. Then he had removed his finger. Some, but not all, of the mercury drained from the tube. The upper part of the tube contained a vacuum.

Debates raged among scientists about why the mercury did not drain completely from the tube. Some thought that a suction pulling on the mercury made it rise. Torricelli claimed that the pressure of the air on the mercury in the dish forced the mercury up the tube. Boyle basically agreed with Torricelli's idea but wanted to explore it further. He set about to expand on the Italian's work.

The Pressure of the Atmosphere

In one experiment, Boyle placed a mercury barometer into the glass bowl of his air pump. As his assistants pumped out the air, the mercury in the barometer fell. Boyle urged his men to continue pumping to see how far the mercury would fall. Despite their efforts, the men could not make the mercury fall below a half inch. Boyle decided that Hooke's air pump, for all its ingenious design, could not produce a perfect vacuum. Enough air still remained to support the half-inch of mercury.

However, he had found proof that it was the pressure of the air, and not the suction of a vacuum, that makes the mercury rise in a barometer. To reinforce the point, he watched carefully as air was pumped back into the bowl. Slowly the mercury in the barometer began to rise.

Another experiment led Boyle to make a remarkable hypothesis about the atmosphere of the Earth. His assistants soldered together a column of tin pipes 32 feet long. The column ended in a three-foot-long glass tube that was then connected to the air pump. Boyle and his assistants stationed themselves on the roof of a four-story theater, with the column of pipes extending down to a vat of water on the ground. Using the air pump, his assistants were able to draw the water up to a height of 33 feet and 6 inches.

Boyle realized that with a perfect vacuum, which his pump could not quite achieve, the water would have been raised to a level of 34 feet. His calculations were based on the differences in size and weight between a 30-inch mercury barometer and the huge "water barometer" he had created. Then he made another calculation. Since water weighs 1,000 times more than the same volume of air, the air around the Earth must rise 1,000 times higher than the column of water produced by the pump. Therefore, the atmosphere must extend at least 34,000 feet, or almost seven miles, above the Earth's surface.

> "Our Boyle is one of those who are distrustful enough of their reasoning to wish that the phenomena should agree with it."
>
> **HENRY OLDENBURG IN A LETTER TO BENEDICT DE SPINOZA**

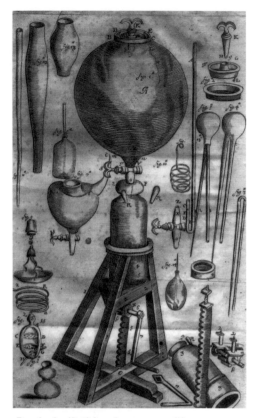

Actually Boyle understood that the atmosphere's total height was doubtless much greater. With less air pressure on them, the upper layers would spread out to even greater heights. Still, Boyle's calculations represented a new picture of the layers of atmosphere that blanket the planet.

Boyle built this air pump with Robert Hooke's help to find out if air had weight.

Weighing Air

Boyle had already studied the weight of air in another ingenious experiment. One night, at a meeting of the Invisible College, an interesting question arose. Does air have weight? The great minds present, such as Sir Christopher Wren, an architect, and Seth Ward, a doctor, pondered the idea but reached no conclusion. Intrigued, Boyle began to design an experiment to answer the question.

With Hooke's help, he put his ideas to work. From a glassblower's shop, he ordered a glass bulb the size of an egg. At one end was a narrow stem through which the pump could operate. First Boyle placed the bulb, which was filled with air, on one pan of a weighing scale inside the bowl of the air pump. Tiny weights were placed on the other pan. Then his assistants pumped out the air. Time and again, Boyle and his men had to open the bowl, add or remove tiny weights, close the bowl, and pump out the air. Finally, Boyle got the scale to balance.

Next, Boyle repeated the procedure but this time with the small bulb also pumped free of air and sealed with wax. The side of the scale with the tiny weights fell, indicating that the bulb weighed more with air inside than without it. At their next meeting, the members of the college were duly impressed by Boyle's remarkable solution.

Isaac Newton experiments with light. Boyle's book New Experiments *inspired the young scientist.*

A Great Book of Science

In 1660, Boyle decided to publish the results of his work with the air pump. The book, titled *New Experiments Physico-Mechanicall: Touching the Spring of the Air and Its Effects*, began with a detailed description of Robert Hooke's design for the air pump itself. Then it proceeded to describe in unprecedented detail 43 experiments that Boyle and his assistants had performed with the apparatus.

> "Boyle was after all one of the most impatient of thinkers when it came to fake or non-explanations, and he was in general very aware of the danger of letting verbal 'explanations' get in the way of real ones."
>
> **J.J. MACINTOSH,
> UNIVERSITY OF CALGARY**

Each experiment was laid out step-by-step so that other scientists could, if they chose, repeat the tests themselves. Prior to Boyle, scientists had followed Aristotle's approach to science, which urged them to look at the world closely but not to experiment. In fact, most thinkers of Boyle's time believed that experiments were "unnatural" and that the results of an experiment would conflict with the way nature actually works. Boyle, however, influenced by Francis Bacon and others, believed that the experimental proof of theories was the best way to advance scientific knowledge. This idea became known as the scientific method.

Boyle's book was an immediate success not only among scientists but also with general readers. It established the 30-year-old Boyle as one of the great natural philosophers of the day. One key to the book's success was its straightforward language. Boyle realized that many of its claims might seem confusing or outrageous to his readers, so he tried to present his findings as simply and clearly as possible.

One who was impressed by Boyle's experiments was an eighteen-year-old student named Isaac Newton. *New Experiments* helped inspire him to do his own groundbreaking work in physics, optics, and other areas. Another of Boyle's early readers was the famous diarist Samuel Pepys. His curious mind was delighted by Boyle's ingenious methods. Pepys resolved to buy every book that Boyle would publish in the future.

Boyle's Law

The scientific law that bears Boyle's name was another result of his work on air pressure. It was published in the second edition of *New Experiments* in 1662. As in his work with the air pump, Boyle relied heavily on Hooke's assistance to complete the experiment.

Boyle began with a long glass tube in the shape of a J. The tube's short leg was sealed and the long leg left open. He poured enough mercury into the tube to trap a pocket of air in the short leg. Tilting the J tube allowed him to get an equal level of mercury in each leg. Boyle measured the height of the air column in the short leg— 48 spaces of ruled paper. As he added mercury to the long leg, he saw the volume of air in the short leg begin to shrink. Finally, the 48 spaces of air were compressed by half, to 24 spaces. Meanwhile, the volume of mercury in the long leg had exactly doubled. In other words, the pressure exerted on the trapped air was twice as much as at the start.

Boyle's law became one of Boyle's most notable discoveries. At a constant temperature, the volume of a gas in a confined space varies inversely with the pressure of the gas: $PV = k$.

An example of this law is the use of a syringe. To draw fluid into a syringe, the plunger is pulled out, which increases the

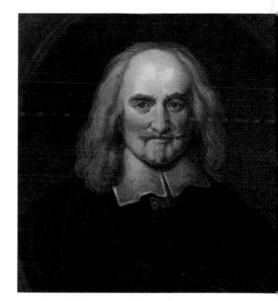

Thomas Hobbes (above) and others attacked the theories Boyle proposed in the first edition of New Experiments, *leading Boyle to publish a second edition of the book.*

volume inside the syringe. Correspondingly, this decreases the pressure on the inside. The outside pressure thus forces the fluid into the syringe. To reverse the action, the user pushes the plunger in. This decreases the inside volume, which increases the pressure and forces the fluid out.

Typically cautious, Boyle himself did not apply his new hypothesis to all gases. He declared that it applied only to air and only under specific circumstances. Nevertheless, Boyle's law remains the first written law to describe the properties of the atmosphere. It affirmed Boyle's notion that the atmosphere—that indeed the whole universe—followed laws that could be discovered and tested.

A Bout with Controversy

Boyle had a good reason for publishing a new edition of his book. Certain readers, including the philosopher Thomas Hobbes, had attacked him for his claims in the first edition. Some doubted whether Boyle had achieved a true vacuum in his work and attributed his results to some other force. Hobbes questioned the scientific method itself and viewed the whole Invisible College with suspicion.

With typical self-control, Boyle replied to the charges by affirming the importance of experiments. In fact, he added more examples of his work on air pressure, such as Boyle's law. In defending this work, he proposed a new theory about what we today call atoms.

Boyle had found that gases could be compressed or expanded much more than liquids or solids. From this, he reasoned that the particles in a gas must have more space between them than the particles in a liquid or solid. These particles Boyle called "corpuscles." Ridiculed by many at the time, Boyle's idea is the foundation for our understanding of matter as the product of tiny particles called atoms and molecules.

The Skeptical Chemist

Between the first and second editions of his book on the air pump, Boyle published another landmark work, *The Skeptical Chymist* (1661). In it, he addressed the basic assumptions about chemistry and matter that had been made since Aristotle.

Aristotle had declared that all the substances in the world were made of some combination of four elements: fire, water, air, and earth. Scientists since then had taken this as a postulate, or first truth. If the results of a chemical experiment did not agree with this postulate, then the experiment had to be flawed.

In his own work, however, Boyle had come to challenge Aristotle's idea—which is why he referred to himself as "skeptical" in his book's title. To begin with, Boyle questioned whether the wide variety of substances on Earth could all be formed from just four elements. Also, he challenged other beliefs related to the four-element theory. For example, the ancients

Aristotle believed that all matter was made of water, air, fire, and earth.

believed that fire always reduced a substance to simpler ingredients. Boyle heated sand, limestone, and soda ash together to form glass, a new compound more complex than the original

Members of the Royal Society meet to discuss science. The organization developed from the former Invisible College.

ingredients. Placed in fire again, the glass melted but did not break down into the original substances.

Boyle's advice to chemists was to replace the old system with a new one based on careful experiments. He also wrestled with his own definition of an element to replace Aristotle's idea, but his notions were as yet too vague. In fact, the writing style of *The Skeptical Chymist* was much wordier and more confusing than the clear text of *New Experiments*. Boyle seemed to be groping for ideas that were just beyond his reach.

The Royal Society

Throughout this period, Robert Boyle continued to meet and correspond with his friends in the Invisible College. His assistant, Hooke, took up new duties for the group. He designed a special experiment to be shown at each meeting. Like Boyle, Hooke had a genius for experimental science, and his demonstrations were always the highlight of the evening.

The group's meetings had become an excellent way to exchange information, theories, and objections. It occurred to the members that their Invisible College should become more formalized. Political problems that had disrupted the group in the past no longer existed. In 1660, with the civil wars at an end, Charles II had been restored to the throne. Later that year, the records of one meeting declared that "the King had been acquainted with the design of this Meeting. And he did well approve of it, and would be ready to give encouragement to it."[4]

The core members of the group included Boyle, John Wilkins, Christopher Wren, Seth Ward, and Henry Oldenburg. Oldenburg, a Puritan known for his fine penmanship, had transcribed Boyle's notes so his books could be published. He became secretary of the new organization. It was decided that membership would not be limited to scientists. Statesmen, clergymen, physicians, peers, poets—all were welcome provided they had an interest in the new natural philosophy. Even Samuel Pepys, Boyle's early champion, joined.

After petitions were sent to the king, the members were granted a royal charter on July 15, 1662. This document gave

King Charles II approved of the Royal Society and became a charter member.

the group the official sanction of the monarchy. The name granted was the Royal Society of London. The king himself became a charter member and attended the first meeting after the grant. The members chose Boyle to conduct a program of experiments for Charles II. He showed how heat caused a natural lodestone to lose its magnetism. He demonstrated how the pressure of air could hold two slabs of marble together

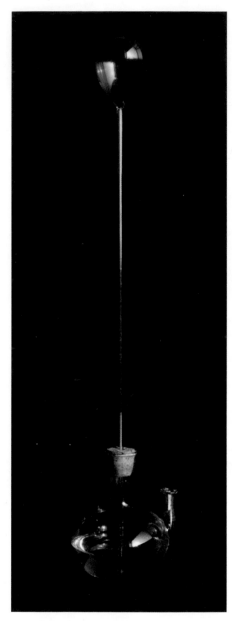

Robert Boyle used Galileo's design to construct this type of thermometer.

even though a weight was hung from the bottom slab. The king was duly impressed.

The Royal Society took as its motto the Latin phrase *Nullius in Verba*, meaning "nothing in words." The founders meant that science should be based on experiments, not on the handed-down words of the ancients. It was a philosophy close to Boyle's heart.

Back to the Laboratory

With Hooke occupied full-time with the society, much of Boyle's work with the air pump came to an end. Still, he did not lack for new areas of interest. Optics, phosphorescence, the properties of heat and cold—these were just some of the phenomena that he explored. Boyle understood and appreciated the complexity of the world, and he believed that it could best be explained by mechanical laws. This was his way of revealing the wonder of God's creation. At a time when science was mostly at odds with religion—as evidenced by

Galileo's punishment by the Catholic Church for his writings—Boyle saw his work as a natural extension of his faith. And he continued to publish books of science alongside books of religious philosophy.

Boyle explored the properties of light and colors, but his work in this area was inferior to that done by Hooke and later by the brilliant young scientist Isaac Newton. Boyle's experiments with heat and cold, however, yielded better results.

To begin, he realized he would need a more accurate thermometer than any currently in use. The air thermometer created by Galileo employed colored water in an open container in which a long glass tube was upended. Warm temperatures heated the air in the tube, causing the air to expand and drive out more of the colored water. In cold weather, however, the water froze, making the instrument useless.

Boyle designed a thermometer filled with colored alcohol that would not freeze in the winter. In addition, he sealed the glass tube, which negated the effects of outside air pressure and made the instrument portable. Boyle's new alcohol thermometer quickly became a popular item among ordinary citizens as well as scientists.

Boyle also found that by mixing salt with crushed ice, he could achieve temperatures far below freezing. He set out to investigate why containers filled with water cracked when the water froze. Boyle's theory was that water, unlike other substances, actually expanded when it froze. To test this idea, he half filled a glass jar with water and placed the jar in a pail of salt water and crushed ice—the subfreezing mixture. Then he filled the pail with regular ice. The bottom half of the jar was thus colder than the upper half. The water in the jar froze from the bottom up, raising the level of the water in the jar. This proved that water did indeed expand when frozen—to about 9 percent greater volume than before.

Another experiment employed the air pump and a container of warm water. The container was placed inside the bowl, the bowl was sealed, and the air was removed. Gradually, the warm water began to boil. Reducing the air pressure had lowered the boiling point of the water.

A bell ringer calls people to bring out their dead during the Black Plague of 1665, an event that brought the Royal Society's work to a halt.

The Plague and the Great Fire

Boyle's world was his laboratory, but he was not exempt from disasters in the outside world. In 1665, the Black Plague struck the city of London. The disease spread rapidly, its victims suffering from fevers and terrible running sores. Once contracted, the plague was a death sentence. Whole families were cut down, buildings and houses were boarded up, and wagons transported piles of bodies to mass graves outside the city.

As a result, members of the Royal Society scattered for their own safety. Boyle's visits to London came to a halt. Even the royal court moved to Oxford to avoid the outbreak. Unfortunately for Boyle, Charles II required his presence at all kinds of court functions. The shy scientist had no love for such events and longed to return to his work. Even in his laboratory, however, he was often interrupted by visitors sent by the king.

The next year, another disaster struck London. An enormous fire began at the house of the king's baker. Overnight, the blaze spread to the docks at the Thames, where coal barges ignited into a firestorm. Choking black smoke covered the city. Hot cobblestones cracked with a sound like pistol shots. For four days, the fire caused havoc throughout London. At the end, huge sections of the city were reduced to smoldering rubble.

Members of the Royal Society played prominent roles in rebuilding the city. The architect Christopher Wren drew up plans and put them into effect. Robert Hooke served as his assistant. As for Robert Boyle, he used his wealth to assist those left homeless by the disaster.

Fire rages through London in 1666. Boyle and other members of the Royal Society helped rebuild the city.

Back to London

For all its recent troubles, London still held an attraction for Boyle. In the autumn of 1668, he decided to return there and live with his sister Katherine in Pall Mall. To curious friends, he explained that London, as the home of the Royal Society, was now the center for natural philosophy. Oxford had been hospitable and a wonderful working environment for more than a decade. The university there had even given him an honorary degree. Still, he felt it was time for a change.

Privately, Boyle had more serious reasons for the move. His health, which had always been delicate, had grown worse. A series of ailments, from kidney stones to stomach problems to malaria, had taken their toll in recent years. Plagued with weak eyes, he now could barely see to correct the proofs of his books. Assistants were hired to read to him deep into the night. He dictated his writings to scribes. Finally, he gave in to Katherine's urgings and placed himself under her care.

Moving the leading chemist of the day was no easy task. Workers carried dozens of crates containing a bewildering array of jars, bottles, retorts, tubes, glass bowls, instruments, and apparatus. More than 3,000 books had to be hauled into his quarters. Soon, however, he returned to work in a laboratory at the back of Katherine's house. Although Boyle's body had grown weaker, his mental energy was undiminished.

> "That then, that I wish for, as to systems, is this, that men, in the first place, would forbear to establish any theory, till they have consulted with . . . a considerable number of experiments, in proportion to the comprehensiveness of the theory to be erected on them."
>
> **ROBERT BOYLE,**
> *EXPERIMENTAL ESSAYS*

French chemist Antoine Lavoisier (pictured) named oxygen as the element necessary for burning and breathing more than 100 years after Boyle theorized about it.

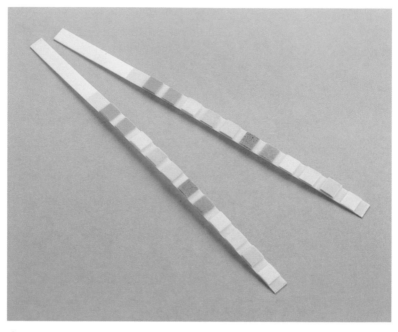

Scientists use strips of paper covered in litmus to show the presence of acid or alkali in a substance. Boyle's litmus test has become a standard part of laboratory science.

The Litmus Test

Some of Boyle's greatest work in chemistry was done over the next few years. He began to analyze substances in a variety of ways to determine their special properties. In fact, Boyle coined the term "chemical analysis." Among the chemical tests he developed were assays for gold and silver, a test for salt in water using silver nitrate, a test of 30 steps for analyzing mineral water, and a test for copper using ammonia.

Another test he devised became a staple of laboratory science. Boyle discovered that a vegetable substance from lichens called litmus could be used as a chemical indicator. When touched with an acid, the indicator changed from blue to red, while alkalis made it turn green. Boyle categorized as neutral those substances that did not change the indicator. He had found a useful method for classifying substances.

Gunpowder Under Water

Boyle also built on the experiments he had carried out at Oxford, always digging deeper to get at root causes. He tried burning sulfur, a chemical found in gunpowder, on a red-hot plate, first in air and then in a vacuum. In air, the yellow sulfur burst into a blue flame. With air removed, the sulfur sent up fumes but refused to ignite. These results led Boyle to test gunpowder, which was a mixture of sulfur, charcoal, and saltpeter, or potassium nitrate. He observed that the gunpowder exploded on the hot plate in air. In a vacuum, it burned.

Boyle's idea that matter was composed of particles called corpuscles came close to describing molecules.

Boyle was at a loss. What was it in gunpowder that allowed it to burn without air? As a further test, he filled the tip of a goose quill with gunpowder, lit it, and dipped the quill in water. The gunpowder continued to burn under water, giving off dark, smoke-filled bubbles.

Boyle theorized that there must be a substance common to both gunpowder and air that allowed for combustion. In related experiments, Boyle had discovered that air contained something that was necessary for respiration, or breathing. Boyle trusted his results but was cautious about jumping to a conclusion. It would be more than a hundred years before a French chemist named Antoine Lavoisier finally named this element that is crucial to burning and to life—oxygen.

Definition of an Element

The more Boyle worked at analyzing substances, the more he refined his view of what matter is. Boyle had already stated his hypothesis—shared by many scientists in his day—that matter was made up of particles that he called "corpuscles." In his *Origine of Forms and Qualities* (1666), he had declared that there was only one kind of "Catholick or Universal Matter,"which took the form of tiny corpuscles of various shapes and sizes. Boyle believed that these corpuscles could join in different clusters to create different substances. Here Boyle was close to describing a molecule, which can be one atom or a cluster of atoms. He was also on the threshold of understanding how changes in the arrangement of molecules cause substances to change—a process called chemical reaction.

> "Robert Boyle . . . a man who alone hath done enough to oblige all Mankind, and to erect an eternal Monument to his Memory."
>
> **JOSEPH GLANVILL, FROM *PLUS ULTRA* (1668)**

In *The Skeptical Chymist*, Boyle had demolished the old Aristotelian notion of the four elements. However, it had always concerned him that he had offered nothing in its place. In the second edition of the book, he added an appendix that contained his definition of an element:

> I now mean by elements, as those chymists that speak plainest do by their principles, certain primitive and simple, or perfectly unmingled bodies; which not being made of other bodies, or of one another, are the ingredients of which all those perfectly mixt bodies are immediately compounded, and into which they are ultimately resolved.[5]

In other words, an element was something that was not a compound or mixture of other substances. Any substance that could be broken down by chemical means was not an element. Boyle also declared that only by experimenting could one determine if something was an element.

Boyle himself played down the importance of his statement. He even referred to the idea as "laboriously useless." But many would say that his definition of an element was the starting point of modern chemistry, which has catalogued the elements in a periodic table and is finding new combinations for them in chemical compounds.

An alchemist works in his laboratory. Boyle communicated with alchemists about creating a way to turn lead into gold.

Study of Alchemy

Throughout the 1670s, Boyle continued to produce a steady stream of books on science, philosophy, and religion. Another of his major interests, however, was an unusual mixture of the three. Like many other natural philosophers of his day, Boyle was fascinated by alchemy.

Alchemy was the forerunner of chemistry. It also contained aspects of magic and mysticism. Since the Middle Ages, alchemists had tried to create the philosophers' stone, an imaginary tool that could change lead into gold. This magical change was called a "transmutation."

Beginning at Stalbridge, Boyle had worked on his own version of the philosophers' stone. In one of his early books, he even described what he believed to be a reverse change of gold into silver. Most of his writings on alchemy, however, were written in code, as were his letters to other alchemists. Boyle feared that if knowledge of how to make the philosophers' stone got out, the results could be disastrous.

Of course, there were links between Boyle's work in alchemy and his chemistry studies. If corpuscles, or atoms, could be arranged in different ways, then one substance could perhaps be changed into another. Nevertheless, Boyle mostly kept his alchemy work private, and he never published a book on the subject.

A Terrible Setback

Aside from scientific work, Boyle kept himself busy with missionary efforts. He sold a land grant he had received from Charles II to pay for a translation of the Bible into the Irish language of Gaelic. He also paid to have Bible translations into Turkish and Arabic. He even joined the East India Company, a group that carried on trade with the East, to help spread his faith among peoples in Asia.

Two years after moving to Pall Mall, however, Boyle suffered a stroke. For months he could barely move or speak. At best he was able to dictate experiments for his assistants to do. Finally, after eleven months, he mustered enough strength to rise from his bed.

Isaac Newton visited Boyle after the older man had recovered from his stroke. The two remained friends until Boyle's death.

King Charles II meets with Christopher Wren, the architect of St. Paul's Cathedral and a friend of Boyle.

Though weakened by the stroke, Boyle continued with his scientific work. His mind was as sharp as ever, and years of poor health had taught him how to budget his strength. He did not lack for eager young disciples to assist him. As it turned out, he published more books in the years just after his stroke than in the period just before it.

Europe's Great Scientist

By now, Robert Boyle had won wide renown for his books, experiments, and theories. No grand tour of Europe was complete without a visit to this great man of science. As soon as his strength returned, he was besieged with callers, from close friends wishing him well to strangers hoping to meet him. Characteristically, Boyle, despite his discomfort in the spotlight, tried to please his visitors. He would show them his latest experiment or a new invention such as the pressure cooker.

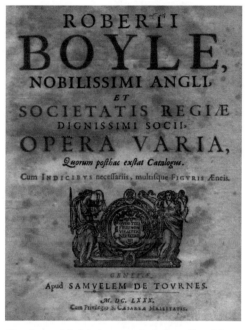

Boyle published more books after his stroke than in the years just before it.

Among his many visitors was Isaac Newton, who shared his love of physics, chemistry, and alchemy. Newton, almost white-haired despite his young age, was honored to meet the great Boyle, a tall, rather frail man with a quiet but friendly demeanor. Newton was just beginning a string of controversies with Hooke over who was first to make certain discoveries. Both Newton and Hooke were considered by many to have

Robert Boyle died on December 30, 1691.

prickly personalities. Yet Boyle remained friends with both to the end of his days.

Soon Katherine began to worry about her brother's health and his work. To placate her, Boyle took steps to give himself more privacy. He rented rooms in an isolated neighborhood where he could go when the press of visitors became too great.

An Honor Declined

Along with the admiration of strangers, Boyle also won honors from his colleagues. In 1680, members of the Royal Society elected Boyle their president. Before taking office, he was asked to sign an oath having to do with precise points of religious faith. Boyle, however, refused to sign a list of points that he had not written himself. Politely, he declined the office. In his place, the society elected Samuel Pepys.

Boyle had often been criticized by other scientists in Europe for not drawing larger conclusions from his experiments. As with the Royal Society oath, his reluctance had to do with his scrupulous sense of truth. He refused to affirm more than he could swear to from his own experience.

Final Years

Boyle continued to work, write, and publish to the end of his life. When he could no longer escape to his rooms across town, his sister Katherine helped him set up visiting hours. He lived to see the completion of his friend Christopher Wren's magnificent St. Paul's Cathedral. He saw London rebuilt as a city of wider thoroughfares and brick structures. Assistants read him Newton's classic book on mathematics and physics, the *Principia*, and Boyle kept up with advances in many branches of science.

In his last decade, he wrote about what he saw as the proper relationship between God and the natural world, and how humans could understand it. The final statement of his philosophy was presented in *The Christian Virtuoso* (1690). Boyle compared nature to a mechanism like a clock. The Creator had set this mechanism in motion at the beginning of time, and it operated now according to natural laws.

These laws, Boyle wrote, could be discovered by science.

Boyle died on December 30, 1691, exactly a week after Katherine's death. He was buried next to his sister in a cemetery that no longer exists. In his will, he funded a series of Christian lectures called the Boyle lectures, which still are given annually. He also left mountains of unpublished papers and journals that gave future scholars even more insight into his thought.

Two days after Boyle's funeral, Samuel Pepys invited a friend to join him in a private tribute to the great scientist. The men symbolically passed Boyle's mantle to his successor, Isaac Newton. They knew that the place of Robert Boyle in the annals of science was secure.

The Great Experimenter

Robert Boyle's main gift to science was his emphasis on experiments. His ingenious methods for testing nature's laws set high standards for others to follow. He published his work, failures and all, in elaborate detail. Having found it disheartening that so few experiments had been recorded in the past, he hoped that his own example would inspire those who came after him.

Although his main interest was chemistry, Boyle managed to make important discoveries in a wide range of scientific fields. His work with Hooke's improved air pump led him to make a series of groundbreaking discoveries about a subject—air—that had scarcely been addressed before. He also described the effects of a vacuum on sound, respiration, and

"For him a God who could create a mechanical universe—who could create matter in motion, obeying certain laws out of which the universe as we know it could come into being in an orderly fashion—was far more to be admired and worshipped than a God who created a universe without scientific law."

J.J. O'CONNER, UNIVERSITY OF ST. ANDREWS IN SCOTLAND

combustion, and showed that air is essential to life.

The tools he introduced to the laboratory included a pocket thermometer, an improved barometer that could indicate weather changes, a hydrometer for measuring the density of liquids, a better method of achieving subfreezing temperatures, a pressure cooker, and even a sulfur-tipped match. He pioneered methods of chemical analysis much like the ones used today.

Among Boyle's many contributions to laboratory science was the barometer.

Influence on His Age

Boyle was an aristocrat in an age that deferred to the privileged classes. His wealth allowed him to devote all his time to his favorite subjects: science, philosophy, alchemy, and religion. His quiet dignity and respected name lent new authority to science as a pursuit.

Perhaps just as important, Boyle distrusted systems and theories that tried to explain too much. At a time when many scientists sought fame by proposing grand systems, Boyle focused on smaller, more certain gains in knowledge. He believed that God had made the universe subject to mechanical laws. All of Robert Boyle's hundreds of experiments were designed to help him discover and describe these laws.

Boyle's many books reached an audience of scientists and ordinary readers around the world. He toppled old beliefs about the nature of matter and offered his own definition of an element and atomic theory. He can rightly be called the father of modern chemistry.

IMPORTANT DATES

1627	Robert Boyle born at Lismore Castle in Ireland, son of the Great Earl of Cork, Richard Boyle.
1635	Boyle and his brother Francis enter Eton, a renowned English boarding school.
1639	Begins grand tour of Europe with Francis and a French tutor.
1640	Undergoes a religious awakening in a thunderstorm.
1641	Tours Italy but fails to meet his hero, Galileo.
1642	Stranded in Geneva because of the Irish Rebellion.
1643	Death of Boyle's father.
1644	Returns to England and is reunited with his sister Katherine; England in midst of civil war.
1645	While living with Katherine, meets members of Invisible College.
1646	Establishes himself at Stalbridge, an estate inherited from his father; writes works of philosophy and theology.
1649	Assembles his own laboratory and begins performing scientific experiments; Charles I beheaded by Parliament.
1652	After Cromwell's defeat of the Irish, receives properties in Ireland that provide him with an income of 3,000 pounds a year.
1654	Moves to Oxford to concentrate on scientific work.
1657	Begins experiments with air pump invented by Robert Hooke.
1660	Publishes *New Experiments Physico-Mechanicall: Touching the Spring of the Air and Its Effects.*
1661	Publishes *The Skeptical Chymist*, containing his refutation of Aristotle's theory of four elements.
1662	Formulates Boyle's law in the appendix to a second edition of *New Experiments*; helps found the Royal Society of London, the oldest continuously active group of scientists in the world.
1665	The Black Plague strikes London.

IMPORTANT DATES

1666	The Great Fire of London destroys huge tracts of the city; Boyle privately uses his wealth to assist the homeless; refines his theory of "corpuscles," or atoms.
1668	Moves back to London for health reasons.
1670	Suffers a stroke and is bedridden for months.
1670s	Continues his work in chemistry and alchemy; sponsors missionary projects in Asia and America; pays for translations of the Bible into several languages.
1680	Is elected president of the Royal Society but declines when asked to sign a religious oath.
1680s	Continues to write and publish on science, philosophy, and theology; receives a steady stream of visitors.
1691	Dies in London shortly after sister's death.

NOTES

1. Quoted in J.J. MacIntosh, "Robert Boyle," *Stanford Encyclopedia of Philosophy*, http://plato.stanford.edu/entries/boyle/index.html.

2. Quoted in J.J. O'Connor and E.F. Robertson, "Robert Boyle," www.gap.dcs.st-and.ac.uk/~history/Mathematicians/Boyle.html.

3. Quoted in J.J. MacIntosh, "Robert Boyle," *Stanford Encyclopedia of Philosophy*.

4. Quoted in "The History of the Royal Society of London," School of Mathematics and Statistics, University of St. Andrews, Scotland, www.gap.dcs.st-and.ac.uk/~history/Societies/RS.html.

5. Quoted in Richard Morris, *The Last Sorcerers: The Path from Alchemy to the Periodic Table*, Washington, D.C., Joseph Henry Press, 2003, p. 58.

GLOSSARY

Alchemy: A mystical study that sought ways to change one substance into another.

Atomic theory: The idea that all matter is made of particles called atoms.

Barometer: A device that measures the pressure of the atmosphere.

Chemical analysis: The process of testing a substance to see what it is made of or what qualities it has.

Chemistry: A science that deals with what substances are made of and how they interact.

Combustion: The chemical process of burning.

Compound: A mixture of substances.

Element: A substance that is not a compound of other substances but is whole in itself.

Experiment: A controlled, step-by-step test designed to reveal something about a natural law.

Natural philosophy: The study of nature and its phenomena; later called simply "science."

Optics: The scientific study of light and vision.

Respiration: The act of breathing.

Scientific method: The use of experiments and observation to gain knowledge.

Vacuum: A space without matter or air.

FOR MORE INFORMATION

BOOKS

Ann Newmark, *Chemistry*. New York: Dorling Kindersley, 2000.

Albert Stwertka, *A Guide to the Elements*. New York: Oxford University Press, 2002.

Salvatore Tocci, *Oxygen*. Danbury, CT: Children's Press, 2004.

Michael White, *Galileo Galilei*. San Diego: Blackbirch Press, 1999.

Chris Woodford and Martin Clowes, *Atoms and Molecules*. San Diego: Blackbirch Press, 2004.

WEB SITES

Robert Boyle
www.gap.dcs.st-and.ac.uk/~history/Mathematicians/Boyle. html. A site by the School of Mathematics and Statistics, University of St. Andrews, Scotland. The site provides a solid narrative history of Boyle's life and work, with links to major topics connected to Boyle and his time.

The Life and Thought of Robert Boyle
www.bbk.ac.uk/boyle/biog.html.
A site maintained by Boyle's biographer Michael Hunter of Birkbeck College, University of London. Contains a detailed account of Boyle's life and work, an examination of his philosophy, and a bibliography.

INDEX

Air, 28, 29, 31–32, 46, 55
Air pressure, 26, 27, 34, 39, 40
Air pump, 6, 8, 25–26, 27,
    29–30, 39, 55
Alchemy, 20, 47–49
Assays, 43–44
Atmosphere, 30–31, 35
Atoms, 35-36, 46

Barometer, 8, 29–30, 30–31, 55
Black Plague, 40–41
Boiling point, 40
Boyle, Katherine, 11, 18, 19, 24,
    43, 51, 53
Boyle's Law, 34–35
Boyle, Robert
  air pressure experiments,
    30–31, 34
  and air pump, 6, 29–30, 39
  and alchemy, 47–49
  early life, 8–13
  and elements, 46–47
  experimental method, 8, 11
  experiments, 20, 21, 33–34,
    37, 40, 53–55
  final years, 51–53
  as full-time scientist, 24
  grand tour, 13–17
  health, 12, 20, 43, 49
  inventions, 8, 40, 51, 55
  and Invisible College, 6, 8,
    22–24
  lectures, 53
  legacy, 8, 53-55
  and litmus test, 43–44

and Royal Society, 38, 51
science and religion, 39, 53
at Stalbridge, 19–20, 21
and vacuum experiments,
    27–29, 55
writings, 20, 32–34, 35–36, 39,
    47, 49, 53

Chemistry, 8, 20, 21, 24, 37,
    43–44, 46, 47
Christian Virtuoso, The, 53
Combustion, 6, 28, 46, 55
Corpuscles, 36, 46

Elements, 46-47
Experimental method, 11
Experiments, scientific, 20, 23,
    33–34, 37-38, 39, 53–55

Galileo, 6, 15, 16–17, 20, 39
Gunpowder, 44, 46

Hooke, Robert, 6, 24–26, 34,
    37–38, 43, 51, 55
Hydrometer, 8, 55

Invisible College, 6, 8, 22–24,
    31, 35, 37

Light, 28, 40
Litmus test, 43–44

Magnetism, 28, 39
Match, sulfur-tipped, 8, 55
Mercury, 30 31, 34

INDEX

Molecule, 46

New Experiments, 32–34, 35, 37
Newton, Isaac, 34, 40, 51, 53

Pepys, Samuel, 34, 38, 51, 53
Physics, 8
Pressure cooker, 8, 51, 55

Royal Society of London, 6,
    37–39, 42–43, 51

Scientific method, 34
Skeptical Chymist, The, 36–37, 46

Sound, 6, 28–29, 55
Stalbridge, 19–20, 21
Subfreezing temperatures, 40, 55
Suction, 26, 30, 31
Syringe, 35

Thermometer, 8, 40, 55

Vacuum, 6, 8, 26, 27–29, 31, 44,
    55

Wilkins, John, 22–24, 38
Wren, Christopher, 32, 38,
    42-43, 53